How You Can Have An Effective
Quiet Time with God Every Day

DAG HEWARD-MILLS

Parchment House

Unless otherwise stated, all Scripture quotations are taken from the King James Version of the Bible.

HOW YOU CAN HAVE AN EFFECTIVE QUIET TIME WITH GOD EVERY DAY

Excerpts from:
Evidence that Demands a Verdict Volume I by Josh McDowell
Published by Here's Life Publishers, Inc. P.O. Box 1576 San Bernadino California 92402
Dake's Annotated Reference Bible
The Power of Faith, Article in October 1999 issue of *Reader's Digest*, author Phyllis McIntosh

All Excerpts Used by Permission

Originally published by Parchment House 2014
under the title
UNDERSTANDING THE QUIET TIME
16th printing 2017

Copyright © 2017 Dag Heward-Mills

First published 2017 by Parchment House
4th Printing 2020

Find out more about Dag Heward-Mills
Healing Jesus Campaign
Write to: evangelist@daghewardmills.org
Website: www.daghewardmills.org
Facebook: Dag Heward-Mills
Twitter: @EvangelistDag

ISBN 978-1-68398-282-1

All rights reserved under international copyright law. Written permission must be secured from the publisher to use or reproduce any part of this book.

Contents

1. The Quiet Time - The Most Important Habit of Your Life 1
2. The Quiet Time – The Secret of Many Great Men 4
3. The Quiet Time – Your Personal Time with God 7
4. The Quiet Time – Your Chance for a Personal Relationship with God 11
5. The Quiet Time - Your Chance to Avoid Shallowness 15
6. The Quiet Time – Powerful Effects of a Quiet Time 19
7. The Quiet Time – Your Chance to Obtain Wisdom 35
8. The Quiet Time – Your Chance for Daily Prayer 39
9. The Quiet Time – Your Chance for Daily Bible Reading and Meditation 50
10. The Master Strategy for Having a Successful Quiet Time 54
11. Seven Steps to an Effective Quiet Time 56
12. Tools for an Effective Quiet Time 61

CHAPTER 1

The Quiet Time - The Most Important Habit of Your Life

"The second half of a man's life is made up of the habits he acquired in the first half."

Dostoyevsky

"The strength of a man's virtues is made up of his habitual acts."

Pascal

A habit is something that you do without thinking about it or intending to do it. Every good Christian has many good habits. These good habits are what have made him into what he is.

All great men have habits that have made them great. Our Lord Jesus had habits that made Him great.

Jesus Christ

1. Going to church regularly

Did you know that Jesus had good habits? The Bible teaches us that He had a habit of going to church on the Sabbath day.

And he came to Nazareth, where he had been brought up: and, AS HIS CUSTOM WAS, he went into the synagogue on the sabbath day, and stood up for to read.

Luke 4:16

2. Going on prayer retreats

Jesus also had a habit of going to a particular garden for retreats. It was a place that He went often. And everyone knew His habit of praying in the garden.

When Jesus had spoken these words, he went forth with his disciples over the brook Cedron, where was a garden, into the which he entered, and his disciples. And Judas also, which betrayed him, knew the place: for JESUS OFTTIMES RESORTED THITHER WITH HIS DISCIPLES.

John 18:1, 2

Daniel

Daniel prayed at specific times of the day. It was something he was used to doing. It was one of the greatest secrets of his life.

Now when Daniel knew that the writing was signed, he went into his house; and his windows being open in his chamber toward Jerusalem, he kneeled upon his knees three times a day, and prayed, and gave thanks before his God, AS HE DID AFORETIME.

Daniel 6:10

Ten Things Every Christian Should Know About Habits

1. A habit is an ACT THAT IS REPEATED EASILY without thinking or planning.

2. A habit is an ACT THAT BECOMES YOUR CUSTOM whether you are conscious of it or not.

3. A habit is often AN INSIGNIFICANT ACT THAT SEEMS TO HAVE NO POWER to affect the future. This is why many people do not recognize the concept of having good habits as a powerful tool for future accomplishments.

4. A habit can EITHER BE GOOD OR BAD, NATURAL OR SPIRITUAL. Spiritual habits are things like morning prayer and having a daily quiet time. Natural habits are things like brushing your teeth and having your daily bath.

5. GOOD HABITS ARE REPEATED AS EASILY AS BAD HABITS.

6. BAD HABITS LEAD TO CONSISTENT FAILURE AND DEFEAT without the person realizing what is happening.

7. GOOD HABITS LEAD TO CONSISTENT SUCCESS AND VICTORY without the person even realizing what he is doing.

8. Bad habits are easy to form but difficult to live with. GOOD HABITS ARE DIFFICULT TO FORM BUT EASY TO LIVE WITH.

9. EVERY SUCCESSFUL CHRISTIAN HAS A NUMBER OF GOOD HABITS THAT have brought him to success. Many years ago, a friend of mine taught me how to have a quiet time with God every morning. I developed that as a personal habit and it has been my greatest secret as a Christian and later as a minister. Almost all the things I preach about come as a result of this good habit.

10. HABITS ARE A SAFETY PROCEDURE FOR CHRISTIANS. This is because even when a leader is under pressure, he will do certain good things habitually, naturally and easily. When under pressure, the leader may not have time to think of what to do or how to act. It is a good habit of prayer or quiet time that may lead him out of difficulty. Just like Jesus, I also have a place I often go to pray. I also often go with my pastors. This habit helps keep me spiritually protected even when I am not aware of danger.

CHAPTER 2

The Quiet Time – The Secret of Many Great Men

Moses Had Quiet Times with God

And the Lord said unto Moses, Hew thee two tables of stone like unto the first: and I will write upon these tables the words that were in the first tables, which thou brakest. AND BE READY IN THE MORNING, AND COME UP IN THE MORNING UNTO MOUNT SINAI, AND PRESENT THYSELF THERE TO ME IN THE TOP OF THE MOUNT. AND NO MAN SHALL COME UP WITH THEE, NEITHER LET ANY MAN BE SEEN THROUGHOUT ALL THE MOUNT; NEITHER LET THE FLOCKS NOR HERDS FEED BEFORE THAT MOUNT. And he hewed two tables of stone like unto the first; and Moses rose up early in the morning, and went up unto mount Sinai, as the Lord had commanded him, and took in his hand the two tables of stone. And the Lord descended in the cloud, and stood with him there, and proclaimed the name of the Lord. And the Lord passed by before him, and proclaimed, The Lord, The Lord God, merciful and gracious, longsuffering, and abundant in goodness and truth, Keeping mercy for thousands, forgiving iniquity and transgression and sin, and that will by no means clear the guilty; visiting the iniquity of the fathers upon the children, and upon the children's children, unto the third and to the fourth generation. And Moses made haste, and bowed his head toward the earth, and worshipped. And he said, If now I have found grace in thy sight, O Lord, let my Lord, I pray thee, go among us; for it is a stiffnecked people; and pardon our iniquity and our sin, and take us for thine inheritance. And he said, Behold, I make a covenant: before all thy people I will do marvels, such as have not been done in all the earth, nor in any nation: and all the people among which thou art shall see the work of the Lord: for it is a terrible thing that I will do with thee.

Exodus 34:1-10

God Commanded Joshua to Have a Daily Quiet Time

This book of the law shall not depart out of thy mouth; but THOU SHALT MEDITATE THEREIN DAY AND NIGHT, that thou mayest observe to do according to all that is written therein: for then thou shalt make thy way prosperous, and then thou shalt have good success.

Joshua 1:8

Adam Had Quiet Times Until He Backslid

And they heard the voice of the Lord God walking in the garden in the cool of the day: and Adam and his wife hid themselves from the presence of the Lord God amongst the trees of the garden. And the Lord God called unto Adam, and said unto him, Where art thou? And he said, I heard thy voice in the garden, and I was afraid, because I was naked; and I hid myself.

Genesis 3:8-10

Prophet Micaiah Knew the Habit of Quiet Time

But Zedekiah the son of Chenaanah went near, and smote Micaiah on the cheek, and said, Which way went the Spirit of the Lord from me to speak unto thee? And Micaiah said, Behold, thou shalt see in that day, when thou shalt go into an inner chamber to hide thyself.

1 Kings 22:24-25

Jesus Had Quiet Times Too

And in the morning, rising up a GREAT WHILE BEFORE DAY, he went out, and departed into a SOLITARY place, and there prayed.

Mark 1:35

Jesus had His personal quiet time "a great while before day". He also taught His disciples to separate themselves from everybody and spend time alone with God.

But thou, when thou prayest, ENTER INTO THY CLOSET, and when thou hast shut the door, PRAY TO THY FATHER WHICH IS IN SECRET; and thy Father which seeth in secret shall reward thee openly.

Matthew 6:6

David Had Quiet Times with God

O God, thou art my God; early will I seek thee; my soul thirsteth for thee, my flesh longeth for thee...When I remember thee upon my bed, and meditate on thee in the night watches.

Psalm 63:1,6

CHAPTER 3

The Quiet Time – Your Personal Time with God

Quiet time is time you spend with God alone. If anybody were to ask me what the greatest secret of my relationship with God is, I would say without any hesitation that it is the power of the quiet times I have with Him everyday. I am eternally grateful to the lady who taught me how to have a quiet time with the Lord every morning. What she taught me has greatly influenced my life to date, and that is why I decided to write this book so that you too can benefit from the power of quiet time.

Seven Things That Happen During Quiet Time

1. **During quiet time you develop the most important relationship of your life.**

   A natural relationship develops between any two people who spend quality time together. Spend quality time with God; Many Christians do not know the importance of this time with God.

2. **Having a quiet time makes you develop the most important personal habit of all time: a regular time with your Creator.**

   I have a quiet time everyday and I spend quality time with the Lord.

3. **During your quiet time you draw near to God and He draws near to you.**

   "Draw nigh to God, and he will draw nigh to you. Cleanse your hands, ye sinners; and purify your hearts, ye double minded."

   James 4:8

4. **A quiet time makes you read the most important book in the world.**

   The Bible is the most important book in the world. It is the most outstanding volume known to the human race.

   Professor M. Montiero-Williams, in comparing other religious books to the Bible said,

   [1]"Pile them, if you will, on the left side of your study table; but place your own Holy Bible on the right side - all by itself, all alone - and with a wide gap between them. For, ...there is a gulf between it and the so-called sacred books of the East which severs the one from the other utterly, hopelessly, and forever ...a veritable gulf which cannot be bridged over by any science of religious thought."[1]

5. **A quiet time is your personal school of the Word.**

   During your quiet time, you sit and learn at the feet of the Greatest Teacher Jesus left us - the Holy Spirit. He will teach you many things and show you many wonderful revelations in the Word.

I have many things to say unto you, but ye cannot bear them now.

Howbeit when he, the Spirit of truth, is come, he will guide you into all truth... and he will shew you things to come.

John 16:12, 13

6. **During your quiet time, you increase in your personal knowledge of the Scriptures.**

   ..add to your faith virtue; and to virtue knowledge.

   2 Peter 1:5

   But grow in grace and in the knowledge of our Lord and Saviour Jesus Christ.

   2 Peter 3:18

   Your personal quiet time gives you the opportunity to add knowledge to your faith.

7. **During your quiet time, you experience the presence of God.**

   Adam experienced the presence of the Lord in the Garden of Eden until he backslid.

   And they heard the voice of the Lord God walking in the garden in the cool of the day: and Adam and his wife hid themselves from the presence of the Lord God...

   Genesis 3:8

   There is a hunger in every man. There is a search in every human being for the presence of God. We all long for the presence of Jehovah. There is nothing like the presence of God. Every preacher longs to feel the presence of God as he ministers.

The church service is never the same without the presence of God. Your life will have fullness of joy as you experience the presence of God in your quiet time!

Thou wilt show me the path of life: in thy presence is fullness of joy; at thy right hand there are pleasures for evermore.

Psalm 16:11

CHAPTER 4

The Quiet Time – Your Chance for a Personal Relationship with God

Not everyone that saith unto me, Lord, Lord, shall enter into the kingdom of heaven; but he that doeth the will of my Father which is in heaven. Many will say to me in that day, Lord, Lord, have we not prophesied in thy name? and in thy name have cast out devils? and in thy name done many wonderful works? And then will I profess unto them, I never knew you: depart from me, ye that work iniquity.

Matthew 7:21-23

One of the least understood statements of Jesus is, "I never knew you." These people were prophesying in His name. They were doing many wonderful works in His name but Jesus said, "I never knew you." I have always wondered how it is possible to do the works without knowing God. Dear friend, you had better believe what Jesus said.

It is possible to be a member and to do great things but not know God. A daily quiet time will make you have a personal relationship with the Lord. Nothing else can make you have a personal relationship with the Lord. Coming to church a thousand times is different from having a personal one to one interaction with the Lord. It is this personal interaction with the Lord which most Christians lack.

It seems that God is more interested in the personal relationship than the great public works that we do in His name. A quiet time will make you have that personal knowledge of God. A daily quiet time will prevent you from going to hell. A quiet time will save you from the delusion that working for God is the same as knowing Him. There are people who work for me but don't know me personally. I have employees who hardly know me. They may recognize me when I come around, but they do not have a personal relationship with me.

I have many shepherds and pastors who work in the church with me. But I do not have a personal relationship with all of them. Definitely, there is a difference between those who just work for me and those who have a personal relationship with me.

How come I have a personal relationship with some of my pastors and shepherds? The answer is simple. Some of these pastors and shepherds make the effort to be close to me and to interact with me personally. Now I know them personally and can even call them friends. There are people in my church who do wonderful works in the name of the church or on my behalf. But the reality is that I don't know them personally.

Earlier on, when someone would ask me how they could do better in the ministry, I would give them twenty-five principles for church growth and then I would show them eighteen strategies for effective evangelism. I might show them seven steps to an excellent ministry. But now, if you ask me that same question I would say just draw closer to God and know Him personally. You see, there is no point in running around on His behalf when you do not know Him personally.

It is time to know Him personally. It is said that pastors worldwide pray an average of seven minutes a day. If the pastors are spending less than ten minutes with their Heavenly Father, then perhaps the ordinary members are spending a few seconds every week with their Lord. It is no wonder the Church is the way it is.

It is time to know Him personally. The only way is to have a regular daily quiet time. Do you expect God to come to you to develop a relationship with you? Certainly not! It is up to you and I to draw near to Him on a daily basis.

Draw nigh to God, and he will draw nigh to you…
James 4:8

In this regard, a daily quiet time may actually be your passport to heaven.

When you meet someone in public and shake his hand you can hardly say you know him. In my home, I have a picture which my mother-in-law took with President Clinton. When she showed it to us, we said, "Wow, when did you meet him? How did you get to know him?"

She smiled and told us about how she had had a brief interaction with him and had taken a picture at a conference. The picture gives an impression that he knows her. But the reality is that he doesn't know her at all, and she doesn't know him either. Meeting someone in public does not mean that you know him at all.

Knowing about someone is different from knowing the person. There are many people who know about me but do not know me.

Some people who see me from afar may have the impression that I am proud. Some people may hear me speak and think that I am a difficult person. May God forgive me for my sins. However, some people who know me personally may have a different impression.

Knowing God from afar is very different from knowing Him personally. Your impressions from afar will only change when you get closer to Him. The way you can develop that personal relationship with God is not in public at the church service. You do not develop a personal relationship with God by attending conventions and crusades. You cannot develop a personal relationship with anyone by interacting in public. There has to be communication at a personal level. There has to be a personal interaction! There has to be a quiet time. You can know God personally by spending time with Him during your quiet time.

CHAPTER 5

The Quiet Time - Your Chance to Avoid Shallowness

And these are they likewise which are sown on stony ground; who, when they have heard the word, immediately receive it with gladness; And have no root in themselves, and so endure but for a time: afterward, when affliction or persecution ariseth for the word's sake, immediately they are offended.

Mark 4:16, 17

Shallowness is the disease of the Charismatic Christian. A lot of talk but no depth. Even our churches are shallow and without depth. A shallow end without depth. I once visited a place near the Sahara desert. I was amazed that there were only a few Charismatic or Pentecostal churches there. You see, for all our noise, we the Charismatic and Pentecostal churches have no real outreach to the places of greatest need. So it is with the Christians. We are loud, noisy, "praisey" people with lots of positive confessions. And yet, there is little depth in most of us. It is time to come out of shallowness.

Seven Symptoms of Shallowness in Christians

1. A lack of knowledge of the Scriptures.

Christians do not know what the Bible says about many things. We conducted an exam in one of our churches. Here came a gentleman who claimed to be a shepherd/leader. I gave him a Bible and said to him, "Show me where the Bible speaks about the resurrection." This gentleman could not find where the Bible talked about the resurrection. This is truly a symptom of shallowness. People are in churches shouting and singing but they have no depth. No wonder Charismatic Christians are easily swayed by the next wave of sensationalism.

2. Inability to quote Scripture.

Quoting Scriptures is different from knowing where things are in the Bible. Any Christian of depth will be able to quote Scriptures. Every Christian should have a version of the Bible from which he quotes accurately.

I was recently preaching in a very large Charismatic church and I began to ask questions. I said to one, "Please quote John 1:12." I said to another, "Please quote 2 Corinthians 5:17." I said to yet another, "What is Romans 6:23?"

Amazingly, most of the Christians who fill Charismatic churches cannot quote these Scriptures. Yet, these are some of the basic scriptures for every believer's foundation.

There can be no progress with God unless we have depth. Scripture memorization is essential. Jesus Christ memorized scripture.

In Matthew 4 when the devil tempted Jesus, He accurately quoted Scriptures from Deuteronomy and paralysed the devil with them.

3. Inability to pray for at least one hour a day.

Shallowness is caused by failure to interact with the Lord. Anyone who has some depth with God spends at least an hour every day in the presence of the Lord. When you know God one hour will be too short for you. Conduct a survey in any large Charismatic church. Ask how many Christians have spent at least one hour in prayer and Bible reading on that day. You will find out that very few people spend more than a few seconds with God. No wonder most of them are shallow and don't know God.

4. Inability to lead and teach after being a Christian for two years.

For when for the time ye ought to be teachers, ye have need that one teach you again which be the first principles of the oracles of God; and are become such as have need of milk, and not of strong meat.
Hebrews 5:12

After someone has been a believer for some time he is expected to also share the things he has received. Paul clearly said that there is a time when a believer is expected to be a teacher. "For when for the time ye ought to be teachers, ye have need that one teach you again…" (Hebrews 5:12).

The failure of the majority of believers to rise into Christian leadership is simply a sign of shallowness in the congregation.

5. A lack of interest in Christian books and tapes.

Shallow Christians rarely read Christian books. A Christian book will take you deeper than you are. It will take you higher in the Lord.

Show me someone who reads Christian books and listens to tapes and I will show you someone who is going deeper with the Lord.

6. Inability to worship God.

I will give you an assignment. Next time you go to church, look around and see how many are singing the songs. Many of the Christians do not even know the songs. They mumble and stumble along as the worship leader leads the congregation. The reality is that they do not know God and have no personal desire to worship Him. It's just a part of the service that has to run its course. They wait for the entertainment that will come from the pastor's jokes. Ask yourself, "Am I a worshipper?" Can you sing the song alone in your home?

7. Inability to fellowship regularly.

The shallowness of many Christians is once again manifested in their inability to regularly fellowship with the Lord and with others.

> **But if we walk in the light, as he is in the light, we have fellowship one with another, and the blood of Jesus Christ his Son cleanseth us from all sin.**
>
> **1 John 1:7**

They struggle to attend church every Sunday and often arrive late. It is almost as though they have a chore to do. Let me ask you a question. When a man is developing a personal relationship with a woman does he not enjoy interacting with her? Does he not long to see her again? The deeper the relationship the greater the interaction will be.

We will have a deep relationship with our God as we have a daily quiet time. Shallowness will be taken away from the church and Christianity will have more meaning for us all.

CHAPTER 6

The Quiet Time – Powerful Effects of a Quiet Time

The reason why many people do not have a quiet time is because they do not know the effect it has on them.

Fifteen Powerful Effects of a Quiet Time

1. **A daily quiet time prevents hurts and reduces pain in this life.**

Much of the pain and hurts of this life would have been avoided if we had used the light of life.

> Then spake Jesus again unto them, saying, I am the light of the world: he that followeth me shall not walk in darkness, but shall have the light of life.
> John 8:12

When a man gropes about in darkness he often hurts himself by bumping into unexpected or unforeseen objects. How painful it is to hit your shin against a table. The pains and hurts we experience in our lives are because we have not picked up the lamp of God.

Thy word is a lamp unto my feet, and a light unto my path.

Psalm 119:105

There will I make the horn of David to bud: I have ordained a lamp for mine anointed.

Psalm 132:17

What is this lamp that God has specially prepared for His anointed ones? It is the Word of God!

The sorrows that some have experienced in marriage have come because they did not use the lamp of God to guide them into marriage. Many people pick up the lamp of God after they have been severely injured by the experiences of life. A lamp is not intended to soothe your pain but to prevent you from getting hurt. How much better a life we would have if we would pick up this lamp on a daily basis. The lamp will keep us from the pain and injuries.

It is only a quiet time that can provide you with constant illumination. If you live in darkness from Monday to Saturday and only receive a little light on Sunday, surely your life will not be the same as someone who lives in constant illumination. Do you want constant illumination for your life? Begin to have a regular quiet time! You will reduce the sorrow of your life by using the true light that God has ordained for you. It is the only light which can light the way for every man on this earth.

That was the true Light, which lighteth every man that cometh into the world.

John 1:9

2. A daily quiet time guarantees a good harvest of nice things.

This is because a daily quiet time is the sowing of spiritual seeds into your spirit. The Word of God is the great seed that you plant in your heart when you have a quiet time.

Now the parable is this: The seed is the word of God.
Luke 8:11

Being born again, not of corruptible seed, but of incorruptible, by the word of God, which liveth and abideth for ever.
1 Peter 1:23

Every time you have a quiet time you are making an investment into your life. You sow the seed of the Word of God and it will yield the fruit of love, peace and joy in the Holy Spirit. Have you wondered why there is little or no love, peace and joy in your life? These fruits can only come as you sow a spiritual seed into your life.

For he that soweth to his flesh shall of the flesh reap corruption; but he that soweth to the Spirit shall of the Spirit reap life everlasting.
Galatians 6:8

Most Christians sow into the flesh. They invest in their flesh. They invest time, money to the development of their flesh and their earthly existence. Others invest seeds of television, pleasure, sex, alcohol and drugs into their flesh. The harvests that comes from such seeds are horrific.

Most pastors are pastoring sheep who live under the devastating effects of a massive harvest from the flesh. It is our duty as pastors to lead the sheep to invest in their spirits on a daily basis.

3. A daily quiet time burns away unwanted things.

When this fire is received on a daily basis, no evil can remain as part of your character.

Wherefore thus saith the Lord God of hosts, Because ye speak this word, behold, I will make my words in thy mouth fire, and this people wood, and it shall devour them.
Jeremiah 5:14

Some things can only be removed by fire. The Word of God is a fire. A daily dose of that fire will take care of every unwanted element in your personality or character.

4. **A daily quiet time breaks down evil strongholds.**

Because a quiet time leads to the breaking and the burning of evil things in our lives, Christians who do not have quiet times often have bad characters. The strongholds in most Christians' lives cannot be broken away by one powerful sermon. Anyone who does not have a regular quiet time has a lot of things that need to be burnt and broken down.

Is not my word like as a fire? saith the Lord; and like a hammer that breaketh the rock in pieces?

Jeremiah 23:29

5. **A daily quiet time leads to the cutting away of unwanted aspects of our lives and character.**

Once again you will see that Christians who just listen to sermons on Sundays but have no regular cutting away of evil tendencies are very different people from those who have a regular quiet time.

For the word of God is quick, and powerful, and sharper than any twoedged sword, piercing even to the dividing asunder of soul and spirit, and of the joints and marrow, and is a discerner of the thoughts and intents of the heart.

Hebrews 4:12

6. **A regular quiet time puts a weapon into the hand of the believer.**

Satan has a good laugh at Christians who are unarmed and exposed. The daily act which Satan hates and fears is when you arm yourself daily with the sword of the Spirit. Prayer is good. Fasting is good. Going to church is good. But none of these can replace the daily arming of God's soldier.

The Word of God has a way of slipping out of our hands. This is because of the pressure of the world in which we live. The opinions of unbelievers, sinners, worldly Christians have a way of eroding the effect of the Word of God on our lives. This is why it is necessary to regularly place the sword into our hands so that we will be ready for every trick of the devil.

And take the helmet of salvation, and the sword of the Spirit, which is the word of God:

Ephesians 6:17

7. Quiet times deliver Christians and pastors from delusions and deceptions about who they are.

It shows us what we are to do to please the Lord.

But be ye doers of the word, and not hearers only, deceiving your own selves.

James 1:22

The prophet Isaiah thought he was good enough. His messages in the first five chapters of Isaiah were very strong against the people. He would often say, "Woe unto them."

Woe unto them that rise up early in the morning, that they may follow strong drink; that continue until night, till wine inflame them!

Isaiah 5:11

Woe unto them that draw iniquity with cords of vanity, and sin as it were with a cart rope:

Isaiah 5:18

Woe unto them that call evil good, and good evil; that put darkness for light, and light for darkness; that put bitter for sweet, and sweet for bitter!

Isaiah 5:20

Woe unto them that are wise in their own eyes, and prudent in their own sight!

Isaiah 5:21

Woe unto them that are mighty to drink wine, and men of strength to mingle strong drink:

Isaiah 5:22

One day, God decided to reveal Himself to Isaiah. Isaiah was shocked when his real condition was revealed by God. All it took was one glimpse of God in His glory. Immediately, Isaiah was delivered from his delusions. He changed his message at once. He said, "Woe is unto me!" He no longer said, "Woe is unto them."

Then said I, Woe is me! for I am undone; because I am a man of unclean lips, and I dwell in the midst of a people of unclean lips: for mine eyes have seen the King, the Lord of hosts.

Isaiah 6:5

As we correct people and see other peoples faults all the time, may God help us to see our own failings. May we see ourselves the way God sees us. Do not be impressed by what people say to you. Do not receive the flattery of human beings. What is highly esteemed in the sight of men is often an abomination in the sight of God.

And he said unto them, Ye are they which justify yourselves before men; but God knoweth your hearts: for that which is highly esteemed among men is abomination in the sight of God.

Luke 16:15

Once I thought I was doing well in the ministry. The Lord revealed Himself to me in a vision and showed me a picture of some greasy faeces. Then He told me that, that was what I looked like to Him. I was full of sorrow for my pathetic condition and I wept before the Lord. I wondered why the Lord had anything to do with me. You see, most people, including myself, thought I was doing well. Dear friend, a regular time with God will save you from delusions.

The Word of God is like that. God shows Himself to you. Every time you read the Word of God, you see God. When Isaiah saw the Lord, he had no deceptions about what he was. Pray that God will reveal Himself to you as you read the Bible everyday. Many church members would not be as proud, arrogant and presumptuous as they are if they knew what they looked like before God. Many Christians would not accuse their leaders if they had just a glimpse at what they were really like in the sight of God.

The Word of God is a mirror. It will show us the real picture. A quiet time will reveal the truth to you every time.

We are so subject to delusions and deceptions that we need a regular input of the Word of God in our lives. I cannot overemphasize the need for regularity for the ministration of the Word in our lives. Only a quiet time can give you the regular input that is needed for a constant deliverance from deception.

8. A daily quiet time will give great spiritual growth.

A daily quiet time exposes you regularly to spiritual food. The Word of God is milk for your soul (1 Peter 2:2). It is bread for the hungry (Matthew 4:4) and it is meat for the men (Hebrews 5:12) and it is sweet honey for the desert.

Charismatic churches are full of thousands of undeveloped spiritual babies. The pastors of today's charismatic churches are seen by their members as superstars who have the answers to everything. This is not the case. Perhaps we pastors enjoy having people depend on us. They look to us as though we are semi-gods with a panacea for every problem.

When I was growing up as a Christian, I belonged to a Scripture Union fellowship. I did not belong to a large charismatic church. There was no superstar TV personality pastor in SU fellowship. We were directed to the Word of God as the source of everything. I am so grateful that the first thing I learnt in the Scripture Union was to have a daily quiet time.

I remember the day I was taught to have a daily quiet time. Little did I know that I was being directed towards the most important thing in Christianity - the Word of God.

I was being shown how to receive milk on a daily basis. Meat and bread for all my needs, and honey when I wanted something sweet.

A spiritual x-ray of a large charismatic church will reveal tiny undeveloped Christians who shout Christian slogans and clichés and hail their pastors as though they were pop stars or soccer heroes. Is it any wonder that Christianity today is a far cry from what it used to be? There is very little sacrifice. There is very little advancement of the kingdom. And there is so much carnality. Carnality is a sign of immaturity. Why is so much of the Body of Christ immature? Because most Christians do not have a daily quiet time.

Christians today depend on a quick microwave snack from their pastors Bible on Sunday morning. Is there any comparison between a child who has a balanced meal every day and someone who has a quick microwave thirty-five minute sermon snack every other week. It's time to grow. It's time to benefit from the milk, bread, meat and honey that is in your Bible. Having a daily quiet time is the best habit I learned as a Christian.

9. A daily quiet time brings inner healing.

He sent his word, and healed them, and delivered them from their destructions.

Psalm 107:20

The Word of God has a way of healing us of our pain and wounds. God will touch you where it hurts if you will allow Him. And He will heal you of every situation in your life.

Spiritual, emotional and psychological problems are the most difficult to solve. Doctors often struggle with these problems to no avail. The diagnosis and treatment of spiritual, emotional and psychological problems are one of the most difficult areas for medicine. But God has a solution. The solution is in His Word. A daily dose of God's powerful Word will bring healing to every inner wound. What did Jesus say? "The Spirit of the Lord is upon me because He has anointed me to preach the gospel and to heal the broken hearted." How was Jesus going to heal the broken hearted? Through the Word of God!

10. A daily quiet time brings healing to the body.

My son, attend to my words; incline thine ear unto my sayings. Let them not depart from thine eyes; keep them in the midst of thine heart. For they are life unto those that find them, and health [medicine] to all their flesh.

Proverbs 4:20-22

The Hebrew word for health is "*marpe*" which means "medicine".

It may sound difficult to believe but God's Word actually brings healing to our physical bodies. The Bible says that they are life and health to the flesh; the flesh means the physical body.

I would like to quote to you a very interesting article I read in Reader's Digest:

[2]*The notion that religious faith can promote physical well-being is not new. Most of us have heard of cases in which someone, seemingly by sheer faith and will, has miraculously recovered from a terminal illness or survived far longer than doctors thought impossible. What is new is that such rewards of religion are becoming the stuff of science.*

"We cannot prove scientifically that God heals, but I believe we can prove that belief in God has a beneficial effect," declares Dale A. Matthew, M.D., associate professor of medicine at Georgetown University Medical Center in Washington, D.C. "There's little doubt that healthy religious faith and practices can help people get better."

Compelling Evidence

Just how powerful is the evidence linking faith and health? More than 30 studies have found a connection between spiritual or religious commitment and longer life. Among the most compelling:

A survey of 5,286 Californians found that church members have lower death rates than non-members, regardless of risk factors such as smoking, drinking, obesity, and inactivity.

Those with a religious commitment had fewer symptoms or had better health outcomes in seven out of eight cancer studies, four out of five blood pressure studies, four out of six heart disease studies, and four out of five general health studies.

People with a strong religious commitment seem to be less prone to depression, suicide, alcoholism, and other addictions, according to one research analysis.

One of the most extensive reviews demonstrates that the connections between religion and health cut across age, sex, cultural, and geographic boundaries. It includes more than 200 studies in which religion was found to be a factor in the incidence of a disease, explains Jeffrey S. Levin, a former professor at Eastern Virginia Medical School in Norfolk. Levin found an association between good health and religion in studies of children and older adults; of U.S. Protestants, European Catholics, Japanese Buddhists, and Israeli Jews; of people living in the 1930's and 1980's; of patients suffering from acute and chronic diseases.

How Prayer Heals

Why does faith appear to have such a powerful protective effect? Experts offer several possible explanations.

Going to religious services guarantees contact with people. Social support is a well-documented key to health and longevity.

Faith gives a sense of hope and control that counteracts stress. "Commitment to a system of beliefs enables people to better handle traumatic illness, suffering, and loss," says Harold G. Koenig, M.D., director of the center for the study of religion, spirituality, and health at Duke University Medical Center.

Praying evokes beneficial changes in the body. When people pray, they experience the same decreases in blood pressure, metabolism, heart and breathing rates as the famous "relaxation response" described by Herbert Benson, M.D. of the Harvard Medical School. Reciting the rosary, for example, involves the same steps as the relaxation response: repeating a word, prayer, phrase, or sound, and returning to the repetition when other thoughts intrude. While the relaxation response works regardless of the words used, Benson says, those who choose a religious phrase are more likely to benefit if they believe in God.

Can Others' Prayers Heal?

Researchers are investigating whether the prayers of others can heal. Benson and his colleagues, studying coronary-bypass patients, and Matthews, studying people with rheumatoid arthritis, are trying to confirm findings of an oft-quoted 1988 study by cardiologist Randolph Byrd, M.D.

Dr. Byrd divided 393 heart patients in San Francisco General Hospital Medical Center into two groups. One was prayed for by Christians around the country; the other did not receive prayers from study participants. Patients did not know to which group they belonged. The group that was prayed for experienced fewer complications, fewer cases of pneumonia, fewer cardiac arrests, less congestive heart failure, and needed fewer antibiotics.

Even more confounding are controversial studies suggesting prayer can influence everything from the growth of bacteria in a lab to healing wounds in mice. "These studies on lower organisms can be done with great scientific precision, and the findings can't be explained away by, say, the placebo effect," says Larry Dossey, M.D., author of Prayer Is Good Medicine.

Doctors as Believers

Dr. Dossey became so convinced of the power of prayer that he began to pray privately for his patients. Nevertheless, he and other experts tread cautiously in this area. "We certainly don't want to start selling religion in the name of science," he says. "People need to make their own choices."

And yet, health care institutions are beginning to pay attention to the faith-health connection. Conferences on spirituality and health have been sponsored by Harvard Medical School and the Mayo Clinic. Nearly half of U.S. medical schools now offer courses on the topic. In a survey of 269 doctors at the 1996 meeting of the American Academy of Family Physicians, 99% said they thought religious beliefs could contribute to healing. When asked about their personal experiences, 63% of doctors said God intervened to improve their own medical conditions.

Clearly, their patients agree that prayer is a powerful tool in healing. Polls by Time/CNN and USA Weekend show that about 80% of Americans believe spiritual faith or prayer can help people recover from illness or injury, and more than 60% think doctors should talk to patients about faith and even pray with those who request it.

This yearning for a connection between religion and medicine is partly a reaction to a health care system that has become increasingly rushed and impersonal. "In medicine, the pendulum had swung so far toward the physical that it almost totally excluded anything spiritual," Dr. Dossey says. "This didn't feel right to patients or many physicians, and the pendulum has begun to swing back."

How Faith Fits In

So what does this mean for the average person? It does not mean adding worship to the list of healthy things you can do. You can't adopt faith as you would a low-fat diet.

What you can do is speak up if you're facing illness or surgery and would like your belief to be part of your health care. That doesn't mean you should expect your doctor to pray with or for you. But it's reasonable to expect him to listen to your needs, arrange a visit from the hospital chaplain, or allow time for prayer before you're wheeled into the operating room.

"Faith" Koenig maintains, "offers people some control over their lives as opposed to just depending on a medical profession that's becoming more distant and mechanized every day."²

11. A daily quiet time causes cleansing.

Now ye are clean through the word which I have spoken unto you.

John 15:3

Sanctify them through thy truth: thy word is truth.
John 17:17

As Isaiah said, "We have unclean lips and we dwell in the midst of unclean people." Thank God that a daily quiet time provides cleansing. Have you ever wondered why there is very little of God's power in the Church today? It is because of the sin and the filth that is in the Church.

For this ye know, that no whoremonger, nor unclean person, nor covetous man, who is an idolater, hath any inheritance in the kingdom of Christ and of God. Let no man deceive you with vain words: for because of these things cometh the wrath of God upon the children of disobedience.

Ephesians 5:5, 6

12. A daily quiet time produces faith in the average Christian.

So then faith cometh by hearing, and hearing by the word of God.

Romans 10:17

Faith comes by hearing and hearing by the Word of God. The more you read the Bible, the more you will believe in God's power to save. The Bible is littered with hundreds of stories of

God's deliverance. You will see people at the brink of death who were saved by God. You will read about people in difficult and complex situations who were saved by the power of God. These testimonies inspire faith. Do not take it for granted. Do not think that you know everything about God. A daily dose of the Word of God will increase your faith.

13. A daily quiet time drives away weariness, dejection and depression.

For as the rain cometh down, and the snow from heaven, and returneth not thither, but watereth the earth, and maketh it bring forth and bud, that it may give seed to the sower, and bread to the eater:

Isaiah 55:10

The Word of God is like rain and snow that cools and refreshes. You will be blessed by the cooling and refreshing effect of a daily quiet time. As I go about I often become weary and unhappy if I have not been able to have time with the Lord. I cannot explain it. You have to experience it for yourself. The refreshing and calming effect that a time in the presence of God produces cannot be compared with anything.

14. A daily quiet time produces power for the ordinary Christian.

For I am not ashamed of the gospel of Christ: for it is the power of God unto salvation to every one that believeth; to the Jew first, and also to the Greek.

Romans 1:16

The Gospel of Jesus Christ (which is the Word of God) is the power of God unto salvation. There is power in the Word of God. There is healing in the Word of God. When you expose yourself to the Word of God you are exposing yourself to a supernatural power. God is actually in His Word. He is the Word. "In the beginning was the Word and the Word was with God and the Word was God." God is the Word or the Word is God.

Expose yourself to the Word and you are exposing yourself to God. The power of God will be real to you.

What power is able to change the lives of thousands of young people who would have been dancing, drinking, smoking and infecting each other with HIV?

I am not talking about elderly men and women without any life or strength. I am talking about young men and women who are changed by the power of God's Word.

Someone once said of my church, "Your church is like a large youth group." You see, my church is made up of mostly young people. I have thousands of young people who serve the Lord with all their heart, might and strength. What has changed the course of their lives? Is it the laying on of hands? Is it fasting? No! It is the Word of God. The Word of God is the power of God with the ability to save and to change.

15. A daily quiet time can make you wiser than your enemies, your teachers and the elders.

Thou through thy commandments hast made me wiser than mine enemies: for they are ever with me. I have more understanding than all my teachers: for thy testimonies are my meditation. I understand more than the ancients, because I keep thy precepts.

Psalm 119:98-100

A daily quiet time will give you the right perspective of life. You will be delivered from delusions about what life has to offer. It will guide you and convert your soul. You will see life from a different perspective. A daily quiet time will make you wiser than the average person around you.

Recently, I was walking on some huge golf courses that belonged to a single Japanese man. As I looked at the vast amount of land that belonged to this gentleman, I hoped that this man knew God. You see, one day he will have to leave this earth and leave the vast properties that he owns.

The Word of God makes you value what is truly valuable. The Word of God makes you see the wealth of this world in the right perspective. Jesus said, "Lay up for yourself treasures in heaven." When the Word of God is in you, you will say to yourself, "I will lay up for myself treasures in Heaven," - that is true wisdom.

CHAPTER 7

The Quiet Time – Your Chance to Obtain Wisdom

1. The quiet time is the key to God's wisdom and therefore to your promotion.

   Wisdom is the principal thing; therefore get wisdom: and with all thy getting get understanding.

   Proverbs 4:7

2. By having a quiet time you exalt wisdom in your life and therefore bring yourself to honour.

   Exalt her, and she shall promote thee: she shall bring thee to honour, when thou dost embrace her.

   Proverbs 4:8

3. A quiet time is your key to wisdom and therefore your key to victory.

   Wisdom is better than weapons of war: but one sinner destroyeth much good.

   Ecclesiastes 9:18

And they were not able to resist the wisdom and the spirit by which he spake.

Acts 6:10

Then shall the lame man leap as an hart, and the tongue of the dumb sing: for in the wilderness shall waters break out, and streams in the desert.

Isaiah 35:6

This book of the law shall not depart out of thy mouth; but thou shalt meditate therein day and night, that thou mayest observe to do according to all that is written therein: for then thou shalt make thy way prosperous, and then thou shalt have good success.

Joshua 1:8

4. A quiet time is your key to becoming wealthy because you have access to the wisdom of God.

   Riches and honour are with me; yea, durable riches and righteousness. That I may cause those that love me to inherit substance; and I will fill their treasures.

   Proverbs 8:18, 21

   Length of days is in her right hand; and in her left hand riches and honour.

   Proverbs 3:16

   The crown of the wise is their riches...

   Proverbs 14:24

5. A quiet time will show you that human cleverness is a poor substitute for the wisdom of God.

   Where is the wise? where is the scribe? where is the disputer of this world? hath not God made foolish the wisdom of this world? For after that in the wisdom of God the world by wisdom knew not God, it pleased

God by the foolishness of preaching to save them that believe. For the Jews require a sign, and the Greeks seek after wisdom: But we preach Christ crucified, unto the Jews a stumblingblock, and unto the Greeks foolishness; But unto them which are called, both Jews and Greeks, Christ the power of God, and the wisdom of God. Because the foolishness of God is wiser than men; and the weakness of God is stronger than men.

1 Corinthians 1:20-25

6. A quiet time makes you move progressively away from human cleverness and towards the wisdom of God.

Let no man deceive himself. If any man among you seemeth to be wise in this world, let him become a fool, that he may be wise. For the wisdom of this world is foolishness with God. For it is written, He taketh the wise in their own craftiness.

1 Corinthians 3:18,19

And it came to pass in those days, that he went out into a mountain to pray, and continued all night in prayer to God. And when it was day, he called unto him his disciples: and of them he chose twelve, whom also he named apostles; Simon, (whom he also named Peter,) and Andrew his brother, James and John, Philip and Bartholomew, Matthew and Thomas, James the son of Alphaeus, and Simon called Zelotes, And Judas the brother of James, and Judas Iscariot, which also was the traitor.

Luke 6:12-16

7. A quiet time introduces you to real wisdom because you begin to fear, respect and obey God.

The fear of the Lord is the beginning of wisdom: and the knowledge of the holy is understanding.

Proverbs 9:10

The fear of the Lord is the beginning of wisdom: a good understanding have all they that do his commandments: his praise endureth for ever.

Psalm 111:10

And unto man he said, Behold, the fear of the Lord, that is wisdom; and to depart from evil is understanding.

Job 28:28

CHAPTER 8

The Quiet Time – Your Chance for Daily Prayer

Quiet time is not only a time of Bible reading and study but also a time of daily prayer. No matter how important you are, you need to communicate daily with the Lord. There are some Christians who only pray but do not study the Word. Such people cannot develop a wholesome relationship with God. It is a combination of the Word and prayer that builds up a daily prayer time.

Eleven Reasons for Daily Prayer

1. Prayer is very important.

Someone once said that it is more important to know how to pray than to have a degree from the university.

There are many things that are important in this life. A good education is important. Money is important. A good marriage is important. But, a good prayer life is most important!

Let this enter your spirit - In all your getting, get prayer! In all your activities, make room for prayer!

2. **Great men like Daniel prayed during their quiet time.**

   Now when Daniel knew that the writing was signed, he went into his house; and his windows being open in his chamber toward Jerusalem, he kneeled upon his knees three times a day, and prayed, and gave thanks before his God, as he did aforetime.

   Daniel 6:10

   You will notice from this Scripture that Daniel prayed three times a day. An important phrase used in this verse is "as he did aforetime". That means that Daniel had been praying these prayers on a regular basis. Daniel was not just praying because he was in trouble; he had a habit of prayer.

   Many times when people become prosperous they stop going for prayer meetings and eventually backslide. Not so with Daniel! He was the Prime Minister of his country, second in authority only to the king. He was a successful man who had risen from slavery to the high office of Prime Minister. He was one of the most respected and feared men in the nation. He was a major politician of the day. He was a civil servant. Yet, he prayed three times a day, every day!

3. **No one is ever too busy, too blessed or too successful to pray.**

   You may have a busy lifestyle and you may be a very important person, however; I do not think that you are busier than Daniel was. Daniel was a Prime Minister, a leader in the nation. Many people think that Heads of State and Ministers of government have a relaxed and enjoyable life, flying all over the world. That is not true!

   I am the head of a large organization myself, and I know that people in high positions do not have an easy life. The higher you go, the greater the responsibility you have.

   There is so much hard work involved in staying on the cutting edge of life and ministry. Did you know that successful executives like Daniel are so stressed out that they are prone to diseases like stomach ulcers and heart attacks? These conditions are more common with very busy people because of the hard work that they do.

Daniel was one such person. He was a Prime Minister, yet he felt that he was not too busy to pray three times a day. If you think you are too busy to pray, then you are deceiving yourself. If you do not pray, it is because you do not want to pray. It is because you do not think that prayer is important now! Daniel was successful, yet he prayed. Why was he able to pray three times a day?

I have watched people in the church rise out of poverty into mega blessings. When they were poor, they had a lot of time to attend prayer meetings. But when they became blessed, they felt everything was all right. No! Everything is not all right! Your state of blessing is not the signal to stop praying!

4. Daily prayer is our source of power and protection.

You must realize that it is prayer that releases the power of God on our behalf. Jesus knew the power of prayer. That is why he spent long hours in prayer.

Maybe you are a successful businessman, and you do not think that you need any of this spiritual "stuff". Perhaps you are a politician and you think your protection must come from fetish or occult powers. Let me tell you right now, there is power in prayer. We do not need any other power when we have the power of prayer. There is protection for us when we pray. The last part of the armor of God is prayer (Ephesians 6:18). In other words, prayer is an important part of your spiritual defense.

In my country Ghana, many people become afraid when they prosper. They feel that somebody may use supernatural powers to try to kill them. You have nothing to fear when you are a prayerful person like Daniel. Many people wanted to kill Daniel. These people did not just think about killing Daniel, they actually plotted to eliminate him. Through the power of prayer, Daniel was protected from the lions.

I see all the lions in your life scattering away in fear! I see your prayer power rising! I see you going forward because of a newfound prayer life!

...that Jesus also being baptized, and praying, the heaven was opened,

Luke 3:21

I see the heavens opening over your life! Never forget this! The heavens opened when Jesus prayed. Both physical and spiritual blessings rain upon you when you are a prayerful person.

5. Daily prayer is important to acquire and sustain the blessings of God.

Do you have anything that you are proud of? Have you achieved anything in this life? Let me tell you that it is by the grace of God. By the power of prayer, you will achieve many great things. It is by prayer that you will sustain what God has placed in your hands.

I know of people who were given thousands of dollars as gifts. Today, that money has disappeared into thin air. God may give you something but it also takes His grace to sustain that blessing. Are you the pastor of a great ministry? Let me tell you, it takes prayer to sustain you in the ministry. Why do you think Jesus kept running away to pray?

There is a law of degeneration at work in the world. Everything is decaying. Your business is decaying. Your church is decaying. Your very life is decaying.

It takes the power of God, through prayer, to preserve everything that God has given to you.

6. Daily quiet time prayer is the most effective because it is habitual.

A man called Dostoyevsky said, "The second half of a man's life is made up of the habits he acquired in the first half."

Pascal said, "The strength of a man's virtues is made up of his habitual acts."

If you are going to be a great person in this life, you need to have good habits. An action becomes a habit when it is repeated many times; sometimes consciously, sometimes unconsciously. It becomes your custom!

Habits can be either good or bad. Remember that good habits are repeated as easily as bad habits.

A good habit will lead to consistent breakthroughs even without intending to. Bad habits will also lead to consistent failure. If you decide to develop a habit of prayer, you are developing a habit for success.

Jesus went to church on the Sabbath because it was his habit. The Bible tells us that Jesus had customs or habits.

…as his custom [habit] was, he went into the synagogue on the sabbath day…

Luke 4:16

Daniel had a custom of praying three times a day.

…he [Daniel] kneeled upon his knees three times a day, and prayed…

Daniel 6:10

Life in the secular world is not designed to include a prayer time. Work starts early in the morning and continues late into the night. Weeks may pass before you even think of prayer. For many people, it is only an impossible situation that reminds them of the need for prayer. Dear friend, it is important for you to include prayer in your life.

God is not a spare tyre! A spare tyre is something that is never used except in emergencies. God is no fool. Whatsoever a man sows, he will reap. If you have time for God on a regular basis, He will have time to bless you on a regular basis. Only the mercy of God makes Him listen to some of our prayers.

Develop your prayer life until it happens spontaneously. Develop your prayer life until you pray habitually without even thinking of what you are doing.

I Made Time to Pray

When I was a medical student, I was very busy with my course work. There was no time to pray at all. But because I had made prayer a part of my Christian life, there was no way I could do without it! I had to somehow include it in my schedule. I decided to pray late at night. I was usually so sleepy that I had to walk about just to stay awake. Prayer was so important to me that I could not leave it out of my life.

One night, as I headed for my room after one of such prayer times, I actually fell asleep whilst walking! It was only when I bumped into the wall of the Spanish Department building of the university that I woke up from my sleep! I believe that God saw my earnest desire to keep praying in spite of an impossible medical school schedule.

7. Quiet time prayer will sustain you in troubled times.

Why do we wait for trouble before we pray? Would you take someone as a serious friend if he only called you when he was in serious trouble? In times of peace, he had no time for you. God is looking for someone who will fellowship with Him in both good and bad times.

The more I preach, the better I become at preaching. The more you pray, the better you will become at prayer. In times of crises, you will find yourself rising up to the occasion and delivering powerful prayers that bring results.

8. Quiet time prayer is needed for national leaders.

There is no doubt that the world is ruled by wicked spirits in high places. The earth is covered with human beings at war with each other on a daily basis. Famine, wars, epidemics and disasters abound! You just have to keep your eyes on the international news and you will hear about another major disaster.

Dictators of all kinds abound in many nations. Like snakes, which shed their skin, many dictators of yesteryear have a new "democratic look" but are still tyrants and despots at heart.

Many national leaders are actually under the influence of evil spirits, and that makes them do the things they do. They cling to power instead of honorably allowing others to have a chance at leadership. Like vampires, they drink the blood of the nation's wealth and stack it away in secret places.

Charismatic leaders like Hitler lead entire nations into initial prosperity, and then eventual destruction through war. I always remember how things changed in South Africa after President De Klerk replaced President Botha. A new leader led to the release of Nelson Mandela and the end of apartheid. It is important for us to pray for these leaders so that our nations prosper. The right person at the helm of affairs will make a lot of difference to our nations. I believe that the presence of a prayerful person like Daniel made a lot of difference to that nation.

9. Quiet time prayer will help you to develop the ability to pray for long hours.

Years ago, the only prayers I knew about were those that the priests read out to us in church. The longest I could pray was thirty to forty seconds and that was when I recited the Lord's prayer. There were three prayers I knew how to pray: The Lord's Prayer, Hail Mary and a Prayer to the Angel of God! However, as I grew in the Lord I learnt how to pray for myself. I can now pray for several hours at a time.

I always remember the first time I prayed for three hours.

I was a student in Achimota School (Prince of Wales College) in Ghana. I was in the midst of a crisis and I needed the intervention of the Lord. I can also remember the first time I prayed for seven hours. I was a sixth former in the same Achimota School. I prayed from 10 a.m. to 5 p.m. I enjoy praying for long hours.

Praying for thirty minutes is almost like no prayer to me. Do not misunderstand me; I am not saying that God does not hear short prayers. I am saying that I have developed the art of praying for long hours like Jesus did. Jesus prayed for three hours in the Garden of Gethsemane.

And he went a little farther, and fell on his face, and prayed… And he cometh unto the disciples, and findeth them asleep, and saith unto Peter, WHAT, COULD YE NOT WATCH WITH ME ONE HOUR? He went away again the second time, and prayed… And he came and found them asleep again: for their eyes were heavy. And he left them, and went away again, and prayed the third time, saying the same words.

Matthew 26:39, 40, 42-44

In this Scripture, Jesus was surprised that the disciples could not pray for one hour.

And he cometh unto the disciples, and findeth them asleep, and saith unto Peter, What, could ye not watch with me one hour?

Matthew 26:40

Jesus prayed all night before He chose His disciples.

And it came to pass in those days, that he went out into a mountain to pray, and continued all night in prayer to God. And when it was day, he called unto him his disciples: and of them he chose twelve, whom also he named apostles;

Luke 6:12, 13

Long prayer may not be an explicit instruction in the Bible, but it is implicit throughout the Word. In later chapters, I will teach you what to pray about when you decide to pray for long hours.

10. Quiet time prayer will help you to develop a very personal relationship with God.

Many Christians can only pray when they are in a group. They cannot stay in a room on their own and pray for one hour. That is a great handicap. There is a difference between praying alone and praying with a group of people. Both types of prayer are important.

If you can pray for three hours on your own then you can pray for six hours with other people. It is easier to pray in a group. Each time, you expand your ability to pray alone, you are expanding your ability to chalk great achievements in prayer.

11. Quiet time prayer will help you to imitate the prayer life of Jesus.

There are four important times to pray: morning, afternoon, evening and all-the-time.

Jesus prayed in the morning and so do I.

And in the morning, rising up a great while before day, he went out, and departed into a solitary place, and there prayed.

Mark 1:35

What is so important about morning prayer? Prayer in the morning is very good because you meet God before you meet the devil. You meet God before you meet the circumstances of life. God anoints you to overcome every mountain that you will encounter in your life.

Prayer in the afternoon signifies prayer in the midst of activities. When you pray in the afternoon, it signifies that in the heat of the day and in the thick of the battle, you recognize God as the most important force in your life. God will bless you for afternoon prayer. I see you praying in the afternoon!

And when he had sent them away, he departed into a mountain to pray.

Mark 6:46

You can take a little time off your lunch break and pray. That prayer will do you more good than a plate of rice will!

It is also important to pray in the evenings. When the Bible says "watch and pray", it does not mean keep your eyes open when you pray. What it actually means is, stay awake and pray.

And it came to pass in those days, that he went out into a mountain to pray, and continued all night in prayer to God.

Luke 6:12

There is something about praying in the night that is different from praying during the day. It is a very different experience. I have heard stories that witches are very active around 2 a.m. in the night. Perhaps when you pray in the night you are tackling the forces of darkness in a different way. After all, they are called the forces of darkness (night).

The fourth important time to pray is "all-the-time".

Pray without ceasing.

1 Thessalonians 5:17

Prayer is intended to be a never-ending stream of communication with your heavenly Father. He has given us the baptism of the Holy Spirit and the gift of speaking in tongues. I pray all the time. My wife tells me that sometimes I pray in my sleep!

Pray without ceasing.

1 Thessalonians 5:17

You can pray on the bus and on your way to work. You can pray softly to yourself when you are in the office. You can pray when you are in the shower. God is happy when His children are constantly in touch with Him.

I have a friend whose wife calls him on his mobile phone at least seven times a day. I have been in meetings with him when he had received not less that four calls from his wife. Nothing important, she was just keeping in touch! I think it is a nice thing. She phones without ceasing!

I see you praying without ceasing! I see you praying in the morning and in the evening! God is changing your life because of your new found prayer life!

Your marriage, business and ministry will never be the same by the time you finish reading this book!

When, like Daniel, you decide to pray for long hours, you will discover that you will need to have a pattern or a formula for prayer. You need something that will guide you in your prayer life.

CHAPTER 9

The Quiet Time – Your Chance for Daily Bible Reading and Meditation

Study to show thyself approved unto God, a workman that needeth not to be ashamed, rightly dividing the word of truth.

2 Timothy 2:15

These were more noble than those in Thessalonica, in that they received the word with all readiness of mind, and searched the scriptures daily, whether those things were so.

Acts 17:11

For whatsoever things were written aforetime were written for our learning, that we through patience and comfort of the scriptures might have hope.

Romans 15:4

Oh, the lost art of Bible study! It is sad to see that many Christians do not even read the Bible. Since many people do not read the Bible, they obviously do not study it. In this chapter, I will show you how you can study the Bible effectively.

Three Types of Bible Study

1. **Microscopic Bible Study** - reading very short passages, meditating on single verses and words, and examining the meanings of these verses and words using the English, Greek and Hebrew dictionaries and concordances.

2. **Topical Bible Study** - this is done by studying individual topics like faith, love, patience and loyalty.

3. **Telescopic Bible Study** - this involves studying the Bible from a broader perspective.

How to Have a Microscopic Bible Study

1. Analyse each single word in the verse you are studying.

2. Find out the meaning of every single word in the verse with a dictionary.

3. Check your Bible for any related verses. Analyse these verses also.

4. Look for any corresponding Greek or Hebrew words and find their deep meanings.

5. Ask yourself the following questions:

    i. What does this verse mean?

    ii. What does this verse mean to me in my specific circumstances?

    iii. What is God telling me personally?

    iv. What is the verse saying?

v. What is the verse not saying?

vi. How can I apply it to my life?

vii. Is there a command for me to obey?

viii. Is there a warning in the verse for me to heed?

ix. Is there a good example to follow and a bad example to avoid?

x. Is there an allegory (story, parable) for me to interpret?

xi. Is there a promise for me to believe?

xii. Is there anything for me to pray about?

xiii. Who can I share this with?

6. Take note of all punctuation and quotation marks.

7. Never take a verse out of context.

How to Have a Topical Bible Study

1. Define the topic using a very good dictionary, e.g., Oxford's or Webster. Any topic can be chosen, for example; patience, zeal or love.

2. Look for all the verses that refer to the topic and read them aloud.

3. Study all these verses microscopically.

4. Find the following:

   i. The "Why" and "Why not" of the topic. For example, "Why have patience?" or "Why not have patience?"

   ii. The "How" and "How not" of the topic. For example, "How do you have patience?"

   iii. The "Where" and "Where not" of the topic. For example, "Where do you practice love?" or "Where don't you practise love?".

- iv. The "When" and "When not" of the topic. For example, "When should you be zealous?" or "When should you not be zealous?"
- v. The "What" and "What not" of the topic. For example, "What is love?" or "What are the things that are not love?" e.g., love is not sex, sex is not love.
- vi. The "Who" and "Who not" of the topic. For example, "Who should you be patient with?" or "Who should you not be patient with?"

5. Look for types of the topic. For example, "What are the types of love?" - phileo, agape and eros.

6. Look for examples of the topic. Look for examples of patience in the Bible. Look for examples of zeal, e.g. Jesus.

7. Look for problems/mistakes related to the topic. What are the problems that come when you don't walk in love? What problems do people have when they don't have patience?

How to Have a Telescopic Bible Study

1. Read a whole book at a time, preferably in one sitting. Because you are reading large sections it would be easier to read more modern versions of the Bible.

2. Build up a complete picture.

3. Locate the central theme, key verses or passages.

4. Do a microscopic Bible study on key words that you come across.

CHAPTER 10

The Master Strategy for Having a Successful Quiet Time

Three Strategies for a Successful Quiet Time

Strategy # 1 - Set a Practical, Unchangeable and Regular Time for Your Quiet Time

Set a regular time when you meet God. It is very important that you set a regular time for your quiet time. Life is such that important things are often overlooked. If you do not schedule a constant period for a quiet time I assure you that you will leave it out. The best time for a quiet time is first thing in the morning.

Notice that Moses had his quiet time in the morning.

And be ready in the MORNING, and COME UP IN THE MORNING unto mount Sinai, and present thyself there to me in the top of the mount. And no man shall come up with thee, neither let any man be seen throughout all the mount; neither let the flocks nor herds feed before that mount.

Exodus 34:2, 3

Strategy # 2 - Withdraw from the Presence of Other People

And no man shall come up with thee...
Exodus 34:3

A quiet time is not a prayer meeting involving all the members of your household. A quiet time is not another church service or fellowship meeting. It is an intimate time between you and your God. It is a private moment that you must cherish. You will notice that Moses could not have his quiet time in the presence of others. A quiet time is a time when you are alone with God. You cannot develop a personal relationship with someone unless you are alone with the person. It must be possible to withdraw yourself from the company of others so that you can be alone with God.

If you can afford it, you must create for yourself a private place in your home where you go to pray and meet with God.

Strategy # 3 - Create an Atmosphere that Is Conducive for Fellowship with God

You can do this by playing good worship music in the background. If you do not have any such music you can worship the Lord yourself. As you worship the Lord, the presence of the Lord will fill your room. God inhabits praises. There is an atmosphere in which God's presence thrives. I find it easier to pray when I am playing worship music or preaching tapes.

There is no need to struggle in an icy and hardened atmosphere. Put on some music and worship the Lord!

CHAPTER 11

Seven Steps to an Effective Quiet Time

Step #1 - Pray to Begin Your Quiet Time

It's time to give the Lord praise and worship for His goodness. Pray thanking the Lord for another day. Thank Him for who He is, what He has done and what He can and will do. Now ask God to speak to you.

And the Lord passed by before him, and proclaimed, The Lord, The Lord God, merciful and gracious, longsuffering, and abundant in goodness and truth, Keeping mercy for thousands, forgiving iniquity and transgression and sin, and that will by no means clear the guilty; visiting the iniquity of the fathers upon the children, and upon the children's children, unto the third and to the fourth generation. And Moses made haste, and bowed his head toward the earth, and worshipped.
Exodus 34:6-8

Open thou mine eyes, that I may behold wondrous things out of thy law.
Psalm 119:18

Step #2 - Read a Passage from the Bible Expecting God to Speak to You

Read the passage for the day expecting God to speak to you from it. There are several ways of choosing your daily Bible reading passage.

How to Choose Your Daily Bible Reading Passage

1. Choose a book from the Bible of which you read a few verses every day.

You must always remember where you ended so you can continue from the same place on the next day. In the New Testament, I have had wonderful quiet times as I have read through the books of Luke and Ephesians. In the Old Testament, I have also had wonderful quiet times as I have read through the books of Genesis and 1st and 2nd Samuel.

2. Choose a personality from the Bible whose life story you follow.

A few verses from passages about Moses will give you much revelation for your life. You must always remember where you end your reading so that you can start the next day from that point.

3. Take the passage suggested in your daily reading guide.

When I first became a Christian, I depended on Our Daily Bread for my quiet time.

Step #3 - Meditate (Think Through and Soberly Reflect on What You Have Read)

If you do not think about what you are reading you will lose a major blessing of the Word of God. Paul told Timothy to think about the Word of God.

Consider what I say; and the Lord give thee understanding in all things.

2 Timothy 2:7

Seven Keys to Effective Meditation

1. **Read the passage slowly.**
2. **Do not read a very long passage unless it is necessary.**
3. **Stop at any verse that strikes you and think about it.**

God's Word is so powerful that only a single word in a verse is enough to change your life. Each quiet time should be a search for that single word that can change your life.

4. **Think about the meanings of the words that you are reading.**
5. **Think about how the Scripture applies to life in your generation.**
6. **Whisper to the Holy Spirit.**

Say, "Help me Holy Spirit to understand your Word. Father, give me the Spirit of Wisdom and Revelation." I have prayed for many years that God should give me the Spirit of Wisdom and Revelation of His Word.

That the God of our Lord Jesus Christ, the Father of glory, may give unto you the spirit of wisdom and revelation in the knowledge of him:

Ephesians 1:17

7. **Decide on a practical way to implement the scriptures that you have learnt.**

Without thinking of a way to apply the scripture directly you will often not benefit from your quiet time.

Step #4 - Move into Deeper Bible Study and Make Further References to Things that Strike You during Your Quiet Time

There are times that you will need to have a longer quiet time. God may minister to you about something. You must be prepared to study further. This is why it is important to have a good reference Bible.

Look through the passage again for as many of the following as possible:

1. What does the passage teach me about the nature of God: the Father, the Son, or the Holy Spirit?

2. Is there a promise for me to believe, and to claim, taking careful note of any conditions attached?

3. Is there a command for me to obey, or a good example for me to follow?

4. Is there a warning for me to heed or a bad example for me to avoid?

5 Is there a prayer for me to pray or remember?

Step #5 - Use Your Bible Reading Guide

You may refer to your daily Bible reading guide. These Bible reading guides are very helpful in developing a regular quiet time habit. You will benefit from anointed teachers whose ministry will help you to grow.

Step #6 - Write Down Whatever the Lord Tells You

It is important to develop the habit of writing the things that God speaks to you about.

The very fact that you have acquired a notebook shows that you have faith in an invisible God. You believe that He has spoken to you and you have written down His words. You have taken a great step of faith. Without faith it is not possible to please God.

Step #7 - Now Spend Time Praying to the Lord. Listen to the Voice of the Holy Spirit

The last step in your quiet time is to pray. At times you will pray for a short time, but there are other times you will pray for a long time. As you have your quiet time regularly, this prayer time will become longer and longer. You will soon desire longer hours with the Lord.

During the prayer time, God will speak to you through His Spirit. There are things God needs to tell you directly through His Spirit. The Holy Spirit is real and you must believe in Him as well.

CHAPTER 12

Tools for an Effective Quiet Time

1. Bibles

You will need several Bibles to have an effective quiet time. Good Bibles to have are: Dake's Annotated Reference Bible (King James Version), Thompson's Chain Reference Bible (King James Version), New International Version, The Amplified Bible and the New American Standard Bible.

The Bible is God's book for us today. As you read it you will hear the voice of God speaking to you. As you study the Word of God, you will discover new revelations which will affect your life.

2. A Notebook

And the Lord said unto Moses, Hew thee two tables of stone like unto the first: and I will write upon these tables the words that were in the first tables, which thou brakest.

Exodus 34:1

You need to write down the things God says to you. I have a book in which I write the things that God shows me. Sometimes I am surprised at the many revelations and instructions that the Lord has given me. I write down the dreams, visions and the words that God gives to me.

3. A Dictionary

Both Oxford and Webster's dictionaries are good dictionaries to have. You will always be surprised to learn the meanings of words which we often assume we know.

4. A Concordance

Every Christian should have a Strong's Concordance since it is exhaustive.

5. A Good Attitude

Recognize God as the author.

God, who at sundry times and in divers manners spake in time past unto the fathers by the prophets, Hath in these last days spoken unto us by his Son, whom he hath appointed heir of all things, by whom also he made the worlds;

Hebrews 1:1, 2

Focus on Jesus as a central figure in the Bible.

Ought not Christ to have suffered these things, and to enter into his glory? And beginning at Moses and all the prophets, he expounded unto them in all the scriptures the things concerning himself.

Luke 24:26, 27

Be willing to receive instructions from the Lord.

All scripture is given by inspiration of God, and is profitable for doctrine, for reproof, for correction, for instruction in righteousness:

2 Timothy 3:16

Allow God to change you.

But we all, with open face beholding as in a glass the glory of the Lord, are changed into the same image from glory to glory, even as by the Spirit of the Lord.

2 Corinthians 3:18

References

Chapter 3

1-1 Excerpts from *Evidence That Demands A Verdict*, Volume 1, p. 15 1B Josh McDowell Published by Here's Life Publishers, Inc.

Chapter 6

2 - 2 Excerpts from *The Power of Faith*, Article in October 1999 Issue of *Reader's Digest*, author, Phyllis McIntosh.